TALK LIKE YOU MEAN IT
COURSE HANDBOOK

LINCOLN COSTELLO

Copyright © 2025 by Lincoln Costello

All rights reserved.

No part of this publication may be reproduced, stored in a retrieval system, or transmitted in any form or by any means —electronic, mechanical, photocopying, recording, scanning, or otherwise without the prior written permission of the author, except as permitted under Sections 107 and 108 of the U.S. Copyright Act of 1976. Requests for permission should be directed to the author at:

lincoln_costello@fitnyc.edu

ISBN-13: 979-8-9985731-3-2

First Edition

Printed in the United States of America

Published by Lincoln James

This textbook is designed for instructional use in public speaking and communication courses. While every effort has been made to ensure accuracy and current best practices, the author assumes no responsibility for any errors, omissions, or consequences arising from the application of the information contained herein.

This publication follows the conventions of the Publication Manual of the American Psychological Association (7th ed.). All third-party material is either reproduced with permission or used under fair use guidelines for educational purposes. Attributions are provided in table and figure notes throughout, with a complete References section included at the end of each chapter in accordance with APA (7th ed.) guidelines.

CHAPTER 1
NARRATIVE SPEECH

1. Required Readings   *Course Handbook* – Intro Materials & Unit I (Welcome!)
Ch. 1 — 4 What Is Public Speaking, Preparing Your First Speech, Managing Speaking Anxiety, Becoming a Better Listener

Ch. 5 & 6 — Understanding Speech Outlines, Crafting Your Outline

Ch. 7 — Understanding Delivery

Ch. 8 — Online Presentations

Sample speeches — BrightSpace site

---

2. Quizzes   *Course Guide*, Chapters 1–8, sample speeches

---

3. Participation Points   Online and in-class activities; PRPSA Research participation; REAL PS 1

---

4. Speech Assignment   Narration

NARRATIVE SPEECH FOCAL AREAS:

TO BEGIN our journey into public speaking, we'll explore four key elements that shape every speaking experience:

- **Research** – Drawing meaningful details from your own experiences.
- **Ethics** – Building credibility and avoiding plagiarism in your speeches.
- **Analysis** – Reflecting on your confidence and abilities as a speaker.
- **Language & Listening** – Engaging fully with your peers through active, open-minded listening (see Chapter 4).

Additional details about these core components are available in your course materials and on BrightSpace. These topics are designed to deepen your understanding of how effective speeches are created and delivered.

SPEECH 1: DELIVERING A PERSONAL NARRATIVE

Your first formal assignment is to share a **true story from your own life** with the class. This is your opportunity to introduce yourself in a memorable way while practicing basic speech structure and delivery.

Storytelling is a powerful way to connect with an audience — it can entertain, inform, or inspire. Professors often use personal stories to illustrate concepts; in the same way, you'll be using your story to help classmates get to know you.

Assignment Guidelines

- Choose **one specific event** from your life that holds personal meaning.
- Clearly explain why this event matters to you — typically in your introduction or conclusion.
- Keep the scope narrow so the story is easy to follow and fits within the time limit.
- No outside research is required for this speech; instead, focus on chronological organization and practicing delivery skills.

This first speech helps you build credibility for future assignments while letting you concentrate on speaking with confidence.

Audience Role

When you're not presenting, you'll play an important role as an **engaged audience member**. You'll practice evaluating others' speeches and offering constructive feedback, which will strengthen your listening skills and help you see different storytelling approaches.

NARRATIVE SPEECH GUIDELINES

Your first formal speech is one you already know how to give—because it's about you. You'll be telling a true story from your own life. This is your chance to connect with your classmates, share something meaningful, and start building your confidence as a speaker.

Step 1: Understanding the Assignment

- **Type:** Personal narrative — a real event that happened to you.
- **Style:** Extemporaneous (prepared, but not read word-for-word).
- **Purpose:** Help your classmates get to know you, while practicing organization and delivery.

Tip: The best stories are specific. Instead of "my summer vacation," try "the night I got lost at the county fair."

Step 2: Choosing Your Story

Your topic should:

- Be a **true event** from your life.
- Carry **personal significance** — explain *why* it mattered to you.
- Be **narrow in scope** so you can tell it well in the time limit.

Step 3: Audience Awareness

- **Who you're talking to:** Your classmates.
- Think about their **age, background, and shared experiences** so you can connect with them.
- Show sincerity and integrity — people listen more closely when they know you're being real.

Step 4: Building Your Speech
Your speech should:

- **Follow chronological order** (start to finish in time sequence).
- Use **vivid, specific details** so listeners can picture the event.
- Include your **autobiographical connection** (why it matters to you).
- Use natural, clear **voice and volume** so everyone can hear.
- Keep **eye contact**, stand with good posture, and match your facial expressions to the mood of the story.

Presentation aids: You must bring a relevant object, as well as focus on your physical presence.

Step 5: Time & Notes

- **Length:** 2 ½ to 4 ½ minutes.
- **Notes:** Use them only as a backup if you lose your place — do *not* read from a script.

Why This Speech Matters
This first assignment sets the tone for the rest of the semester. You'll be practicing:

1. Storytelling techniques.
2. Audience connection.
3. Speaking without heavy reliance on notes.

As an audience member, you'll sharpen your listening and feedback skills while learning more about your classmates.

CHOOSING YOUR NARRATIVE SPEECH TOPIC

Understanding the Assignment
For your first speech, you'll focus on telling a story from **one specific moment in your life**—not a full autobiography or "greatest hits" list. You can find examples of effective narrative speeches in the course textbook and on BrightSpace, which will give you a clearer picture of expectations.

Finding the Meaning

This assignment asks you to share a story with **autobiographical significance**—something that mattered to you on an emotional level. The event you choose might have been surprising, funny, inspiring, awkward, or even a little unsettling. Whatever the tone, it should be something you can discuss without becoming overwhelmed by emotion. If an experience is still too raw or painful, it's better to choose another memory so you can focus on delivering your speech with confidence.

Keeping the Scope Manageable

Big life milestones are tempting topics, but they're usually too broad to fully explain in the time you'll have. Instead, focus on one clear, memorable event that your audience can relate to. Think along the lines of:

- A memorable family tradition or a quirky relative's habit.
- Your first day at a new school or job.
- A single afternoon when something unexpected happened during a trip.
- A lighthearted mishap, like getting lost or a playful prank gone wrong.

For instance, instead of describing your entire vacation in Italy, you could tell the story of the day you got hopelessly lost in Rome without a map.

Choosing a Recent Event

Stories from the past year or two are often easier to tell vividly, since the details are still fresh in your mind. The more sensory details you can recall, the easier it will be to bring your audience into the moment.

Connecting Rather Than Preaching

When you explain why your story matters to you, aim to connect with your audience instead of teaching them a lesson. Avoid phrases like "The moral of the story is…" and focus instead on sharing how the experience shaped you or revealed something about your personality.

Brainstorming Ideas

Start by writing down at least ten possible topics—don't stop to judge or edit your ideas, just let them flow. Here are a few prompts to get you going:

- An adventure with a friend, sibling, or roommate.

- A "first day" in a new environment (college, job, neighborhood).
- A memorable family tradition, holiday, or outing.
- A meaningful or humorous moment involving a pet.
- A favorite place and something that happened there.
- A harmless prank or practical joke.

Once you've made your initial list, try adding a few more ideas after talking with friends or family—they might remind you of moments you've forgotten.

Narrowing Your Options

Look over your brainstorming list and choose **three possible stories** that you'd enjoy telling. Hold each one up to the assignment requirements:

- Can you describe the moment vividly in just a few minutes?
- Does the story naturally form a beginning, middle, and end?
- Could you include a small object or prop that ties into the story?

Once you've weighed your options, choose the one that feels most engaging for both you and your audience.

Gathering the Details

You're not writing the full outline yet—just jotting down memory triggers. Think of:

- **People** – Who was there? What stood out about them?
- **Setting** – Where did it happen?
- **Senses** – What did you hear, smell, see, feel, or taste in that moment?
- **Atmosphere** – Was it tense, joyful, awkward, exciting?

These notes will help you **re-create the scene** for your listeners when you speak.

FROM IDEA TO DELIVERY

Invention – Shaping Your Idea

- Select a topic that fits the assignment.
- Consider what your audience might connect with.
- Identify key moments or images that will bring the story to life.

Arrangement – Structuring the Story

- Arrange your events in chronological order.
- Build an engaging introduction, smooth transitions, and a clear conclusion.

Style – How You'll Tell It

- Choose words that match the tone of your story.
- Use sensory details so listeners can "experience" the event with you.

Memory & Delivery – Bringing It to Life

- Choose a prop or object that connects to your story (see Ch. 15 in your textbook for inspiration).
- Practice telling the story out loud.
- Use brief notes or cue cards if needed—avoid reading word-for-word.

Connected Writing Assignments
Along with your speech, you'll also:

- Write a brief presentation plan.
- Provide thoughtful feedback on your classmates' speeches.

The M.A.P. Method: Your Guide to Successful Presentations

Think about the last time you prepared for something important — maybe a job interview, a visit to a college campus, or even a weekend getaway. Chances are, you mapped it out in some way. You might've checked the route, made a packing list, or looked up local spots to visit. Could you have just "winged it"? Sure. But your chances of success — and your peace of mind — went way up when you had a plan.

The same goes for planning an oral presentation. A M.A.P. gives you a clear direction and keeps you from getting lost along the way. By making three key decisions early, you set yourself up to arrive at your "destination" confident, prepared, and ready to deliver.

M – Message
Ask yourself: *What's the core idea I want my audience to walk away with?*

- Summarize it in a single sentence or phrase.
- This is your presentation's "big takeaway" — the one thing they'll remember.
- Your message may evolve into the thesis for your speech or report.

A – Audience
Decide *exactly* who you're speaking to.

- Be specific: Are they classmates? Professionals? Volunteers?
- Consider what they already know, what they care about, and what they need from you.
- Tailor your material to them — skip the vague "general public" approach.

P – Purpose
Determine *why* you're sharing this message.

- Are you aiming to inform, persuade, inspire, or entertain?
- Narrow your general purpose into a focused, specific goal.
- You can use brainstorming or freewriting to clarify your purpose before moving forward.

Once you've made these three decisions, you'll have a filter for all your ideas — anything that doesn't fit your M.A.P. can be left out. This keeps you on track and ensures your presentation follows a clear, intentional route from start to finish.

COUNTDOWN TO PRESENTATION – PREPARATION CHECKLIST

In the Days Before Your Speech
- ☐ Review assignment guidelines and grading rubric/critique forms.
- ☐ Finalize presentation plan (MAP + keyword outline).
- ☐ Prepare notes (keywords only, large text, plenty of white space).
- ☐ Create or gather presentation aids (only show when relevant).
- ☐ Rehearse with notes and aids, timing yourself.
- ☐ Avoid memorizing word-for-word—practice for a conversational tone.
- ☐ Decide on outfit: clean, neat, comfortable, slightly more formal than audience.

. . .

The Night Before Your Speech
- ☐ Complete final rehearsal.
- ☐ Visualize a confident, successful delivery.
- ☐ Organize all materials (slides, handouts, critique forms, notes).
- ☐ Get a full night's sleep.

On the Morning of Your Speech
- ☐ Eat breakfast or a light meal.
- ☐ Arrive early to class.
- ☐ Use square breathing to stay calm while waiting your turn.
- ☐ Focus on classmates' speeches (especially those you'll critique).
- ☐ Confirm all digital materials are submitted/uploaded before class.

When It's Your Turn to Present

1. Breathe and smile (if appropriate).
2. Pause before beginning and start at a slow, clear pace—your audience is adjusting to your voice.
3. Increase pace naturally as the audience engages.
4. End confidently—avoid saying "that's it" or anything that downplays your conclusion.

SPEECH CRITIQUES – GIVING AND RECEIVING FEEDBACK

Why Critiques Matter

Peer critiques are valuable not only for the person delivering the speech, but also for the person evaluating it.

- **For Speakers:** Feedback from classmates—whether during the early stages of speech development or after a final presentation—can be incredibly insightful. We tend to focus on what we *intended* to say in our outline, slides, or delivery, rather than what the audience actually *heard*. Classmates can identify gaps, ask clarifying questions, and point out areas that may not flow logically. Multiple perspectives offer a clearer understanding of how the speech is received and where it can be improved.

- **For Reviewers:** Providing feedback is more than just a class requirement—it builds skills in observation, analysis, and professional communication. By evaluating others, you sharpen your ability to identify what works, what doesn't, and how to suggest improvements tactfully. These are valuable skills in both academic and professional settings.

· · ·

How to Offer Helpful Feedback

It's common for students to feel unsure about their qualifications to critique others—or to hesitate because they don't want to hurt feelings. Remember, a critique reflects one person's perspective, and the speaker can choose which suggestions to apply.

As you develop your listening and analysis skills, you'll become better at spotting both strengths and weaknesses in a presentation. Be clear, honest, and respectful. Highlight what worked well so the speaker can build on it, and point out areas for growth in a constructive way. Avoid extremes—being overly harsh or overly flattering doesn't help the speaker progress.

Completing Peer Critiques
- **Before the speech:** Review the critique form in advance so you know exactly what to look for.
- **During the speech:** Take notes discreetly—avoid distracting the speaker—and keep your eyes on them so you can assess body language, eye contact, and delivery.
- **After the speech:** Finish your comments promptly while the details are fresh in your mind. The more specific you are, the more helpful your feedback will be.

Missed peer critiques cannot be made up later. If you are absent, you will lose the participation points for that activity.

Receiving Feedback
- **Instructor Feedback:** Expect to receive comments on both your strengths and areas that need improvement. If something is unclear, ask questions.
- **Peer Feedback:** Accept feedback with an open mind. Even if your classmates are not experts, they are experienced audience members who can provide valuable insight. Appreciate their honesty and encouragement.

Using Feedback to Improve

When preparing for your next speech, look for repeated patterns in the feedback you've received. If multiple people point out the same issue, that's a strong signal that it needs attention. Keep your critique forms and refer to them when planning and practicing your next presentation.

SPEECH CRITIQUE COMPONENTS

When giving or receiving a critique, it helps to know exactly what areas are being evaluated. Below are the general categories your instructor will explain in detail so you'll understand both how you'll be assessed and how to assess others.

(Based on The Competent Speaker Speech Evaluation Form, 2nd ed., by Sherwyn Morreale, Michael Moore, Donna Surges-Tatum, and Linda Webster.)

Part I: Message Preparation

1. **Topic & Audience Connection**
    - Choose and narrow your topic so it's a good match for the audience and the occasion. The subject should feel relevant, timely, and engaging.
2. **Thesis / Specific Purpose**
    - Clearly state your main idea or purpose, making sure it's appropriate for your audience and fits the context of the presentation.
3. **Support**
    - **Supporting Material**
        - Use examples, evidence, details, and reasoning that are credible and suited to your audience.
    - **Presentation Aids**
        - Incorporate visual or audio aids (such as slides, props, or handouts) that enhance—not distract from—your message.
4. **Organization**
    - Structure your speech with a pattern that fits your topic and purpose.
        - **Introduction:** Capture attention, connect with the audience, and preview the main points.
        - **Body:** Use transitions to guide the listener smoothly from one idea to the next.
        - **Conclusion:** End with impact—leave the audience with something memorable.

Part II: Message Delivery

1. **Language**
    - Use words that fit the audience, purpose, and occasion. Keep your tone and word choice clear, inclusive, and appropriate.
2. **Vocal Variety**
    - Adjust your rate, pitch, and volume to maintain interest and emphasize key points.
3. **Vocal Accuracy (Intelligibility)**
    - Speak clearly with correct pronunciation, grammar, and articulation so the audience can easily understand you.
4. **Physical Delivery**
    - Use body language and movement to reinforce your message:

- Eye contact that engages the whole audience
- Facial expressions that match the content and tone
- Natural gestures and purposeful movement
- Posture that conveys confidence and openness
- Effective use of notes and visual aids
- Appearance appropriate for the setting and audience expectations

Managing Your Course Responsibilities

At the start of the semester, you created a calendar of all major due dates. While this course only meets in person for three hours each week—giving you flexibility in how you manage your time—it also follows a precise schedule. Staying on top of deadlines is part of the trade-off for the freedom you have outside the classroom.

Preparing for Class

Many assignments are designed to guide you toward a successful speech, such as brainstorming topics, analyzing your audience, or creating outlines. These are typically due online before class begins, and you'll earn participation points for completing them. Doing these tasks on time ensures you arrive prepared to present confidently.

If you arrive without having completed a preparatory assignment, your instructor may still accept it within one day—but with a penalty equal to one letter grade. Skipping these steps can make your speech preparation much more difficult.

Attendance Matters

Being present is essential—not only because you'll be delivering your own speeches, but because you're part of the audience for your classmates. Listening, providing feedback, and observing other speakers are key parts of the learning process. You'll earn participation points for your engagement during these sessions.

Missed Speeches

Due to the limited number of speaking slots, there are no make-up opportunities for missed presentations. If you miss your scheduled speech date, you'll receive a zero for that assignment, and failing to deliver all assigned speeches will result in failing the course.

In the event of a serious emergency—such as hospitalization or another significant crisis—you may be able to make alternate arrangements if your absence is officially documented through your Dean's Office. Notes from a doctor, emails from family members, or messages from roommates will not be accepted in place of Dean's Office documentation.

Staying on Track

In addition to speeches, you'll complete online quizzes, homework, apprehension reports, and midterm assessments. These activities help reinforce skills, measure your growth, and prepare you for graded presentations.

Strong time management is essential—not just for this class, but for your other courses and your future career. If you need strategies for staying organized, speak with your instructor or visit campus resources, many of which offer free workshops and one-on-one support.

PRESENTATION PLAN – KEYWORD OUTLINE – NARRATIVE SPEECH

Use this template as a guide for creating your own typed keyword outline.

Remember — this is not a full sentence outline. Your instructor will review this plan as part of your "message preparation" grade.

MAP:

- **Message:** _____
- **Audience:** _____
- **Purpose:** To inform / socialize

Introduction *(Write this section in full sentences)*

- **Attention-getter:** _____
- **Why it matters (Relevance):** _____
- **Thesis:** (Set the tone and focus of your story without revealing every detail)
- **Transition to first main point:** *(Write the full transition phrase here)*

Body *(Keyword format)*
I. Rising Action (First Main Point)

- Set the scene, introduce the main characters, and present the challenge or conflict.
- Sensory details and setting go here.

Transition: *(Write the full transition phrase here)*
II. Climax (Second Main Point)

- Deliver the most intense or important moment of the story.
    - A. Supporting point
        - Detail
        - Detail
    - B. Supporting point
        - Detail
        - Detail

Transition: *(Write the full transition phrase here)*
III. Falling Action (Third Main Point)

- Show how the conflict resolves or begins to resolve.
    - A. Supporting point
        - Detail

- ■ Detail
  - B. Supporting point
    - ■ Detail
    - ■ Detail

Transition to conclusion: *(Write the full transition phrase here)*
Conclusion *(Write this section in full sentences)*

- **Restate thesis:** _____
- **Memorable ending:** _____

Notes:

- You may have 3–4 main points, but they don't have to be the same length.
- The rising action often requires the most development, while the falling action is typically shorter.
- Your submitted final outline counts toward 10% of your speech grade.

Use the following pages to critique the students in your critique group. These pages must be turned in for participation points. Peer critiques cannot be made-up in the event of an absence.

Narrative – Critique Form

Speaker _____

Missing, Ineffective, Satisfactory, Good, Excellent **Notes**

Competencies	Part I: Message Preparation – Appropriate for speaker, topic, audience, occasion, and purpose	M	I	S	G	E
Topic	* Chooses and **narrows** a topic					
	Meets general purpose – to inform					
Support/ Organization	* Uses narrative organization pattern (Rising action—climax—falling action)					
	Intro – Uses attention-getter; identifies topic & purpose; establishes relevance; transitions to 1st main point					
	Body – Provides appropriate supporting material with **vivid and specific details**					
	* **Chronological order** with **transition statements**					
	Conclusion – Restatement of thesis; memorable thought that provides closure					
	Part I: Overall					
	*Part II **Energetic** Message Delivery – Appropriate for audience, occasion, and purpose*	M	I	S	G	E
Language	Uses appropriate language for the designated audience; conversational styling					
Voice	* **Variety** – Uses vocal variety in volume, rate, pitch & intensity to heighten and maintain interest.					
	Accuracy – Uses pronunciation, grammar, & articulation; minimizes filler words					
Physical Behaviors	**Appearance and manner** – Dressed appropriately. Appears calm and collected.					
	Movement and gestures – Uses movement and gestures effectively. No roots. No T-Rex arms.					
	Facial expression and eye contact – Uses facial expressiveness and eye contact with classmates to support their message and engage with listeners.					
	Notes – Appropriately designed notecards; Effectively uses notes to support speech.					
	* **Presentation aid** -- Effectively presents personal object to the class.					
Time?	*Part II: Overall*					

* Focal points for this speech – addressed in reading and homework

Notes:

Narrative – Critique Form

Speaker _____

Missing, Ineffective, Satisfactory, Good, Excellent   *Notes*

Competencies	Part I: Message Preparation – *Appropriate for speaker, topic, audience, occasion, and purpose*	M	I	S	G	E
Topic	* Chooses and **narrows** a topic					
	Meets general purpose – to inform					
Support/ Organization	* Uses narrative organization pattern (Rising action—climax—falling action)					
	Intro – Uses attention-getter; identifies topic & purpose; establishes relevance; transitions to 1st main point					
	Body – Provides appropriate supporting material with **vivid and specific details**					
	* **Chronological order** with **transition statements**					
	Conclusion – Restatement of thesis; memorable thought that provides closure					
	Part I: Overall					
	*Part II **Energetic** Message Delivery – Appropriate for audience, occasion, and purpose*	M	I	S	G	E
Language	Uses appropriate language for the designated audience; conversational styling					
Voice	* **Variety** – Uses vocal variety in volume, rate, pitch & intensity to heighten and maintain interest.					
	Accuracy – Uses pronunciation, grammar, & articulation; minimizes filler words					
Physical Behaviors	**Appearance and manner** – Dressed appropriately. Appears calm and collected.					
	Movement and gestures – Uses movement and gestures effectively. No roots. No T-Rex arms.					
	Facial expression and eye contact – Uses facial expressiveness and eye contact with classmates to support their message and engage with listeners.					
	Notes – Appropriately designed notecards; Effectively uses notes to support speech.					
	* **Presentation aid** -- Effectively presents personal object to the class.					
Time?	*Part II: Overall*					

* Focal points for this speech – addressed in reading and homework

Notes:

Narrative – Critique Form

Speaker _____

Missing, Ineffective, Satisfactory, Good, Excellent   *Notes*

Competencies	Part I: Message Preparation - Appropriate for speaker, topic, audience, occasion, and purpose	M	I	S	G	E
Topic	* Chooses and **narrows** a topic					
	Meets general purpose – to inform					
Support/ Organization	* Uses narrative organization pattern (Rising action—climax—falling action)					
	Intro – Uses attention-getter; identifies topic & purpose; establishes relevance; transitions to 1st main point					
	Body – Provides appropriate supporting material with **vivid and specific details**					
	* **Chronological order** with **transition statements**					
	Conclusion – Restatement of thesis; memorable thought that provides closure					
	Part I: Overall					
	Part II Energetic Message Delivery – Appropriate for audience, occasion, and purpose	M	I	S	G	E
Language	Uses appropriate language for the designated audience; conversational styling					
Voice	* **Variety** – Uses vocal variety in volume, rate, pitch & intensity to heighten and maintain interest.					
	Accuracy – Uses pronunciation, grammar, & articulation; minimizes filler words					
Physical Behaviors	**Appearance and manner** – Dressed appropriately. Appears calm and collected.					
	Movement and gestures – Uses movement and gestures effectively. No roots. No T-Rex arms.					
	Facial expression and eye contact – Uses facial expressiveness and eye contact with classmates to support their message and engage with listeners.					
	Notes – Appropriately designed notecards; Effectively uses notes to support speech.					
	* **Presentation aid** -- Effectively presents personal object to the class.					
Time?	*Part II: Overall*					

* Focal points for this speech – addressed in reading and homework

Notes:

CHAPTER 2
CONCEPT SPEECH

1. Required Readings	*Course Handbook* – Unit II
	Ch. 9 – Delivering Informative Speeches
	Ch. 10 – 12 Choosing a Topic & Purpose, Creating Your Thesis Statement, Crafting Strong Introductions
	Ch. 13 – Mastering Vocal Delivery
	Ch. 14 – Finding & Using Sources Ethically
	Ch. 15 – Presentations Pt. 1: Using Visual Aids
	Sample Speeches – BrightSpace
2. Quizzes	*Course Guide*, Chapters 9–15, sample speeches
3. Participation Points	Online and in-class activities; REAL PS 2
4. Speech Assignment	Concept

CONCEPT SPEECH FOCUS AREAS:

- **Research:** Finding credible, reliable sources
- **Ethics:** Presenting accurate information to non-specialist audiences
- **Analysis:** Considering your audience and setting before speaking
- **Language & Listening:** Using clear, accessible language for listeners who are new to the topic

In academic and professional settings, speakers are often tasked with explaining new ideas or clarifying concepts that are misunderstood. Doing this well involves thoughtful research, ethical communication, audience awareness, and clear language. In this assignment, you will practice applying these skills through your **Concept Speech**.

SPEECH 2: TEACHING A CONCEPT

For your next major speaking task, you will prepare a speech that explains a concept connected to your field of study **or** to the college experience in general.

In your first speech, you told a personal story — an experience that relied solely on your own memory and followed a simple chronological structure. For this speech, the challenge is more complex: you'll need to gather information from multiple sources, arrange it in a logical order, and deliver it concisely.

In the real world, whether speaking to clients, colleagues, or employers, the ability to present information clearly and efficiently is highly valued. As a student, you already have emerging expertise in certain areas — now you'll practice breaking that knowledge down so that someone completely new to the topic can understand it as easily as if it were taught in an introductory class.

Your Goal

- Choose a concept related to your academic discipline **or** campus life that genuinely interests you.
- Present it in a way that would make sense to students encountering the topic for the first time.

Things to Consider

- **Audience Needs:** What background information do they need before they can understand the topic?
- **Clarity Strategies:** Could examples, comparisons, or analogies make the explanation more engaging?

- **Research:** Which trustworthy sources will strengthen and support your points?
- **Credibility:** Even if you are familiar with the topic, citing external sources reinforces trust and authority.
- **Organization:** How will you arrange your ideas so that your listeners can easily follow along?

Speech Requirements
Your presentation must include:

- A clear **introduction** that captures attention and sets up the topic
- A well-structured body with distinct, logically ordered **main points**
- Smooth, purposeful **transitions** between ideas
- A **conclusion** that reinforces your message and leaves a lasting impression

CONCEPT SPEECH GUIDELINES

Your second formal speech builds on the skills from your first, but with more complexity. Instead of telling a personal story, you'll explain a concept — one connected to your major or to the college experience — in a way that's clear, accurate, and engaging for newcomers.

Step 1: Understanding the Assignment

- **Type:** Concept speech, delivered extemporaneously (planned in advance but not read word-for-word).
- **Level of Difficulty:** This is a step up from your first speech, requiring research, structure, and integration of outside sources.
- **Purpose:** To inform your audience about a concept, program, or idea in higher education or your field of study.
- **Audience:** Imagine you're speaking to students in an introductory course in your major.

Step 2: Choosing and Focusing Your Topic
Your topic should:

- Be connected to your discipline or to campus life.
- Interest you enough to research and present confidently.
- Be narrow enough to explain clearly in the time limit.

. . .

Step 3: Building Credibility
You will be expected to:

- Use your perspective as a student to help your audience understand the topic.
- Cite at least **two credible sources** — both in writing and out loud during your speech. (Missing oral citations will lower your score.)
- Use a mix of definitions, analogies, and examples to explain your points.

Step 4: Organizing Your Speech

- Use a **topical** or **spatial** structure to arrange your ideas logically.
- Open with a strong introduction and close with a clear, memorable conclusion.
- Use transitions to guide your listeners from one idea to the next.

Step 5: Voice, Language, and Delivery

- Speak with vocal variety and clarity.
- Use language your audience can easily understand — avoid jargon unless you explain it.
- Integrate both vocal and physical delivery strategies (eye contact, posture, gestures).
- Manage any technology smoothly.

Step 6: Presentation Aids

- Use a simple visual aid — for example, two PowerPoint slides with one image each (plus spacer slides if needed).
- Avoid text-heavy slides; let your visuals support your words, not replace them.

Step 7: Time & Notes

- **Length:** 3 ½ – 5 ½ minutes.
- **Notes:** Minimal keyword notes are allowed — do not read from a full script.

Why This Speech Matters

This assignment pushes you to explain complex ideas in a way that's approachable and engaging. You'll be practicing:

- Breaking down information for non-experts.
- Balancing research with clear communication.
- Organizing content for maximum impact.

PREPARING AND DELIVERING YOUR SPEECH

A strong presentation comes from both careful planning and confident delivery. The process can be broken into four stages:

1. Generating Ideas (Invention)

- Select a topic that is well-suited to your audience and occasion.
- Identify what your listeners already know and what they need to learn.
- Gather examples, evidence, and explanations from trustworthy sources.

2. Structuring Your Message (Arrangement)

- Arrange your points into a logical sequence so they are easy to follow.
- Develop a speaking plan that includes a clear opening, purposeful transitions, and a conclusion that reinforces your main idea.
- Consider how each section flows into the next.

3. Choosing Your Language (Style)

- Select wording that connects with your audience's level of knowledge and interest.
- Match the level of detail to your listeners' needs — enough to engage, but not overwhelm.

4. Practicing and Presenting (Memory & Delivery)

- Prepare any visual or digital aids that will support your points.
- Rehearse with your notes and presentation tools until you feel confident.
- Deliver your talk using your prepared materials as guides, not scripts.

Related Written Components

- Submit a phrase or keyword outline of your presentation along with a correctly formatted reference list in APA, MLA, or Chicago style.
- Provide constructive peer evaluations of classmates' speeches.

SELECTING A TOPIC FOR THE CONCEPT SPEECH

When selecting your topic, aim for something you can explain clearly to non-experts while showing depth in your understanding. The process might include:

- Drawing on concepts from your field of study or professional experience.
- Conducting additional research to provide fresh insight.
- Identifying a theory, model, or term that would be new and engaging for a general audience.

Brainstorming prompts:

- Which concepts from your introductory courses were most memorable?
- What recent developments or research have emerged in your discipline?
- Are there new tools or technologies advancing your field?
- What specialized terms or theories from advanced classes stand out?
- Which ideas originally drew you into your field of study?

Review your course materials, textbooks, or reputable journals to expand your list. Aim for at least 10 possibilities before narrowing your choice.

Narrowing Your Focus

After brainstorming possible ideas, start refining your list:

- Consult a variety of credible sources to ensure your understanding is well-rounded.
- Select a topic you genuinely care about — enthusiasm will help you connect with your audience.
- Identify one specific aspect of a broader subject. For example, instead of covering all of climate change, you might focus solely on *urban heat islands*.
- Add supporting visuals, such as charts, graphs, or photographs, to make your explanation clearer and more memorable.

Once you have your list, narrow your focus with inspiration from the sample speech on BrightSpace. As demonstrated there, a broad subject like "lightning" can be distilled into a single, intriguing point of focus.

Research Strategies (See Ch. 14 & p. 124)

- You may use your course textbook as one of your sources.
- Consider conducting an interview with a faculty member who specializes in your topic.
- Explore library databases to locate scholarly journal articles within your field.
- Keep accurate notes and follow the correct documentation guidelines outlined in our textbook (APA, MLA, or Chicago).

Giving Credit in Your Speech – Oral Citations (See Ch. 14 & Ch. 26)

Since your listeners won't have your written bibliography, you must identify your sources aloud. Doing so:

- Enhances your credibility.
- Demonstrates thorough research.
- Shows that you've drawn on more than one reliable source.

Oral Citation Guidelines:

- Clearly state the source's type, title, author, and date of publication.
- Introduce the citation naturally within your speech. For example: *"According to Dr. Maria Sanchez in her 2023 article in Nature Climate Change titled…"*

Organizing Your Material (See Ch. 11 & Ch. 21)

Consider one of these organizational structures for your concept speech:

- **Topical** – divide the subject into related categories.
- **Spatial** – organize based on location or direction.
- **Cause–Effect** – explain how one factor influences another.

Using Visual Aids (See Ch. 15)

For this assignment:

- Select 1–2 strong, image-based visuals (e.g., photo, chart, diagram) that directly enhance your points.
- Limit slides to the image, a short title, and a small-font source credit.
- Avoid bullet points or large amounts of text.
- Even if you modify an image, include the original source.

Tips for Slide Integration:

- Use blank slides (spacer slides) between images for smooth transitions.
- Introduce each visual, pause briefly so the audience can process it, then continue.
- Maintain eye contact — avoid reading directly from the slide.

PRESENTATION PLAN – KEYWORD OUTLINE – CONCEPT SPEECH

Use the following outline as a guide when preparing your concept speech. Your typed, completed outline will be submitted prior to speech day and will be evaluated as part of your **"message preparation"** grade.

MAP:

- **Message:** _____
- **Audience:** _____
- **Purpose:** To inform

Introduction *(Write this section in full sentences)*

- **Attention-getting strategy** (see p. 98 of the textbook):
- **Topic and purpose** (see Ch. 10):
- **Motivating the audience:**
  - Explain why the topic matters to them / addresses an interest or need (p. 100).
  - Establish your credibility as a speaker (p. 99).
- **Thesis statement with preview of main ideas** (see Ch. 12):

Transition to First Main Point: *(Write out the complete transition sentence.)*
Body *(Use keywords and phrases here — no full sentences.)*
I. _____ *(First main point)*

- **A.** Supporting point
  - Detail
  - Detail
- **B.** Supporting point
  - Detail
  - Detail

Transition: *(Write out your full transition sentence.)*
II. _____ *(Second main point)*

- **A.** Supporting point
  - Detail
  - Detail
- **B.** Supporting point
  - Detail

○ Detail

Transition: *(Write out your full transition sentence.)*
III. _____ *(Third main point)*

- **A.** Supporting point
   ○ Detail
   ○ Detail
- **B.** Supporting point
   ○ Detail
   ○ Detail

Transition: *(Write out your full transition sentence.)*
Conclusion *(Write this section in full sentences)*

- See **Ch. 23** for guidance on crafting a memorable ending.

Bibliography: Place your bibliography at the bottom of this page. Follow the correct format for APA or Chicago style as outlined in the textbook.

Concept Speech – Critique Form

Speaker _____

Missing, Ineffective, Satisfactory, Good, Excellent **Notes:**

Competencies	Part I: Message Preparation – Appropriate for speaker, topic, audience, occasion, and purpose	M	I	S	G	E
Topic	Chooses and narrows a topic					
	Meets general purpose – to inform					
Support/ Organization	Uses an organization pattern					
	*Intro – Uses attention-getter; identifies topic & purpose; establishes relevance & credibility; **previews main points**; transitions to 1st main point					
	*Body – Provides appropriate supporting material with vivid and specific details – use of testimony, facts, examples					
	*use of transitions within the speech					
	*Presentation aid – Design of effective presentation aid with spacer slides					
	Conclusion – Restatement of thesis; memorable thought					
	Part I: Overall					
	Part II Energetic Message Delivery – Appropriate for audience, occasion, and purpose	M	I	S	G	E
Language	Uses appropriate language for the designated audience					
	*Effective Oral citation of sources C1 C2					
Voice	*Variety – Uses vocal variety in volume, rate, pitch & intensity to heighten and maintain interest.					
	Accuracy – Uses pronunciation, grammar, & articulation; minimizes filler words.					
Physical Behaviors	*Manner, movement and gestures – Uses movement and gestures effectively					
	*Eye contact and Facial expression – Uses facial expressiveness and eye contact to support the message and engage with listeners					
	Notes – Effectively uses appropriately designed notes to support speech					
	Presentation aid – Effectively presents presentation aid to enhance message					
Time?	*Part II: Overall*					

Notes:

Concept Speech – Critique Form Speaker _____

Missing, Ineffective, Satisfactory, Good, Excellent **Notes:**

Competencies	*Part I: Message Preparation – Appropriate for speaker, topic, audience, occasion, and purpose*	M	I	S	G	E
Topic	Chooses and narrows a topic					
	Meets general purpose – to inform					
Support/ Organization	Uses an organization pattern					
	* **Intro** – Uses attention-getter; identifies topic & purpose; establishes relevance & credibility; **previews main points**; transitions to 1st main point					
	* **Body** – Provides appropriate supporting material with vivid and specific details – use of testimony, facts, examples					
	* use of transitions within the speech					
	***Presentation aid** – Design of effective presentation aid with spacer slides					
	Conclusion – Restatement of thesis; memorable thought					
	Part I: Overall					
	*Part II **Energetic** Message Delivery – Appropriate for audience, occasion, and purpose*	M	I	S	G	E
Language	Uses appropriate language for the designated audience					
	*Effective Oral citation of sources C1 C2					
Voice	***Variety** – Uses vocal variety in volume, rate, pitch & intensity to heighten and maintain interest.					
	Accuracy – Uses pronunciation, grammar, & articulation; minimizes filler words.					
Physical Behaviors	***Manner, movement and gestures** – Uses movement and gestures effectively					
	*ns**Eye contact and Facial expression** – Uses facial expressiveness and eye contact to support the message and engage with listeners					
	Notes – Effectively uses appropriately designed notes to support speech					
	Presentation aid – Effectively presents presentation aid to enhance message					
Time?	*Part II: Overall*					

Notes:

Concept Speech – Critique Form

Speaker _____

Missing, Ineffective, Satisfactory, Good, Excellent **Notes:**

Competencies	Part I: Message Preparation – Appropriate for speaker, topic, audience, occasion, and purpose	M	I	S	G	E
Topic	Chooses and narrows a topic					
	Meets general purpose – to inform					
Support/ Organization	Uses an organization pattern					
	* Intro – Uses attention-getter; identifies topic & purpose; establishes relevance & credibility; **previews main points**; transitions to 1st main point					
	* Body – Provides appropriate supporting material with vivid and specific details – use of testimony, facts, examples					
	* use of transitions within the speech					
	*Presentation aid – Design of effective presentation aid with spacer slides					
	Conclusion – Restatement of thesis; memorable thought					
	Part I: Overall					
	Part II Energetic Message Delivery – Appropriate for audience, occasion, and purpose	M	I	S	G	E
Language	Uses appropriate language for the designated audience					
	*Effective Oral citation of sources C1 C2					
Voice	*Variety – Uses vocal variety in volume, rate, pitch & intensity to heighten and maintain interest.					
	Accuracy – Uses pronunciation, grammar, & articulation; minimizes filler words.					
Physical Behaviors	*Manner, movement and gestures – Uses movement and gestures effectively					
	*Eye contact and Facial expression – Uses facial expressiveness and eye contact to support the message and engage with listeners					
	Notes – Effectively uses appropriately designed notes to support speech					
	Presentation aid – Effectively presents presentation aid to enhance message					
Time?	*Part II: Overall*					

Notes:

Concept Speech – Self-Critique Form   Your Name _____

Missing, Ineffective, Satisfactory, Good, Excellent *Notes*

Competencies	Part I: Message Preparation – Appropriate for speaker, topic, audience, occasion, and purpose	M	I	S	G	E
Topic	Chooses and narrows a topic					
	Meets general purpose – to inform					
Support/ Organization	Uses an organization pattern					
	* **Intro** – Uses attention-getter; identifies topic & purpose; establishes relevance & credibility; **previews main points**; transitions to 1st main point					
	* **Body** – Provides appropriate supporting material with vivid and specific details – use of testimony, facts, examples					
	* use of transitions within the speech					
	***Presentation aid** – Design of effective presentation aid with spacer slides					
	Conclusion – Restatement of thesis; memorable thought					
	Part I: Overall					
	Part II *Energetic* **Message Delivery** – *Appropriate for audience, occasion, and purpose*	M	I	S	G	E
Language	Uses appropriate language for the designated audience					
	*Effective Oral citation of sources C1 C2					
Voice	***Variety** – Uses vocal variety in volume, rate, pitch & intensity to heighten and maintain interest.					
	Accuracy – Uses pronunciation, grammar, & articulation; minimizes filler words.					
Physical Behaviors	***Manner, movement and gestures** – Uses movement and gestures effectively					
	***Eye contact and Facial expression** – Uses facial expressiveness and eye contact to support the message and engage with listeners					
	Notes – Effectively uses appropriately designed notes to support speech					
	Presentation aid – Effectively presents presentation aid to enhance message					
Time?	*Part II: Overall*					

Notes:

CHAPTER 3
PROGRESS REPORT

1. Required Readings	*Course Handbook* – Unit III
	Ch. 16 – Professional Presentations in the Workplace
	Ch. 17 – 21 Speaking with Ethics, Understanding Audience Expectations, Language That Resonates, Delivery with Movement, Understanding Various Organizational Patterns
	Ch. 22 – Presentation Aids Pt. 2: Designing with Intention
	Ch. 23 – Writing Powerful Conclusions
	Ch. 24 – Handling Q&A Sessions with Confidence
	Sample Speeches – BrightSpace
2. Quizzes	*Course Guide*, Chapters 16–24, sample speeches
3. Participation Points	Online and in-class activities; Midterm; REAL PS 3
4. Speech Assignment	Progress Report

PROGRESS REPORT FOCUS AREAS:

- **Research:** Integrating personal expertise with authoritative, credible sources to strengthen your credibility
- **Ethics:** Sharing accurate, relevant details to give a truthful view of the project's status
- **Analysis:** Evaluating your audience and context to determine which updates will be most meaningful
- **Language & Listening:** Tailoring your wording to your stakeholders and preparing to address questions during Q&A

In both academic and professional contexts, progress reports are a way to keep stakeholders informed and engaged. Crafting an effective report means choosing content with care and delivering it in a way that builds trust. Ethical communication is essential—these reports are more than formalities; they shape decisions, timelines, and expectations. Accuracy and transparency aren't just good practices—they're responsibilities.

SPEECH 3 – GIVING A PROGRESS REPORT

For your third major speaking assignment, you will prepare and deliver a **progress report** to an audience of interested listeners. Choose a project you are directly involved in—this could be an ongoing research effort, planning for an event, or a campus initiative such as a policy change or new construction.

What Is a Progress Report?

A progress report communicates the current status of a project, often as part of a longer-term plan. It's a common format in both academic and professional settings. Examples might include:

- A city official updating the community on a public works project
- A marketing manager sharing campaign performance with leadership
- A faculty member reporting on grant-funded research progress
- A software developer presenting updates to a client

Progress reports can be **scheduled** (required at set points in a project) or **unscheduled** (offered proactively to keep stakeholders informed). They may be given at the start, midpoint, or conclusion of a project—and may be delivered in writing, orally, or both.

Your Ethical Responsibility

When delivering a progress report, **accuracy and transparency are essential**. Your audience relies on you to present a balanced account of achievements, challenges, and next steps.

Overemphasizing positives or leaving out setbacks can lead to poor decision-making and damage credibility.

Why This Matters

The ability to give a clear, honest, and well-structured progress report is a skill valued across industries. This assignment will help you practice providing meaningful updates to stakeholders in a **professional and realistic setting**—a skill you'll likely use throughout your career.

PROGRESS REPORT SPEECH GUIDELINES

Your third formal speech builds on everything you've practiced so far, with an even higher level of complexity. Instead of simply explaining a concept, you'll deliver a structured, ethical, and engaging **progress report** — the kind used in real-world academic, professional, and organizational settings.

Step 1: Understanding the Assignment

- **Type:** Progress report, delivered extemporaneously (planned in advance but not read word-for-word).
- **Level of Difficulty:** Level 3 — builds on Levels 1 and 2, adding stakeholder focus, audience analysis, and ethical considerations.
- **Purpose:** To inform stakeholders about the current status of a project you have worked on or are currently working on.
- **Audience:** A group of stakeholders or interested parties who need to know your project's progress.

Step 2: Choosing and Focusing Your Topic

Select a project that you have personal experience with — for example:

- A class project
- Volunteer work
- A professional or workplace project

Your focus should be:

- Narrow enough to explain clearly within the time limit.
- Relevant to your audience's needs.
- Supported by both your personal involvement and credible outside sources.

Step 3: Building Credibility
You will be expected to:

- Use your personal expertise as a participant in the project.
- Incorporate **at least two credible sources** (websites, interviews, articles).
- Cite sources both in writing (bibliography) and orally during your speech.

Note: Missing or insufficient oral citations will result in a point deduction.
Support may include:

- Examples
- Testimony
- Facts and/or statistics

Step 4: Organizing Your Speech
Choose a structure that best fits your report:

- **Chronological** — walk your audience through the project's timeline.
- **Topical** — break your report into major themes or aspects.

Always:

- Open with a strong, clear introduction.
- Close with an effective, memorable conclusion.
- Use transitions to guide your audience smoothly from one section to the next.

Step 5: Voice, Language, and Delivery

- Use language appropriate to your audience — avoid jargon unless you explain it.

- Speak with clarity and vocal variety.
- Incorporate both vocal and physical strategies (gestures, posture, facial expression).
- Manage technology confidently and without distraction.

Step 6: Presentation Aids

- Use **2–4 PowerPoint slides** (plus spacer slides if needed).
- Keep slides visual and concise — they should enhance, not repeat, your speech.

Step 7: Time & Notes

- **Length:** 4 ½ – 6 minutes + Q&A.
- **Notes:** Minimal keyword/phrase notes only — no reading from a script.

Why This Speech Matters

Progress reports are a professional reality in nearly every field. This assignment will help you practice:

- Reporting accurately and ethically to an audience of stakeholders.
- Balancing personal insight with credible, sourced information.
- Presenting complex information clearly and persuasively.

SPEECH PREPARATION AND DELIVERY

Delivering a successful presentation requires both **planning** and **practice**. For this assignment, you'll work through the following stages:

1. Invention

- Select a topic that is relevant, focused, and appropriate for the setting
- Identify your audience and consider what they need or want to know
- Gather supporting material from your own knowledge and reliable, credible sources

2. Arrangement

- Create an introduction that follows the progress report format
- Build a clear, logical speech plan to guide your delivery

3. Style

- Use language that matches your audience's knowledge level
- Select details that are relevant, specific, and engaging for your listeners

4. Memory & Delivery

- Prepare effective visual aids, such as PowerPoint slides, to support your points
- Rehearse with attention to vocal variety, pacing, and slide timing
- Present with minimal reliance on notes, using concise keyword prompts instead of full sentences

Related Writing Tasks

- A **presentation plan/outline** to organize your ideas
- **Peer critiques** to reflect on and learn from others' presentations

CHOOSING YOUR TOPIC

For this assignment, select a project that you are—or have been—personally connected to. This could be through a class, a student group, a volunteer effort, a job, or an initiative that impacts either the FIT campus or the New York City community. Examples include:

- A construction or renovation project
- The rollout of a new policy
- The work of a committee focused on a specific goal or challenge

Your progress report can focus on a project that is:

- In its early stages
- Actively underway
- Recently completed

Brainstorming Possible Topics

Create a list of at least **five** projects you have worked on or contributed to. As you brainstorm, write down every idea—don't overthink or filter too soon. Consider the following categories for inspiration:

- **Academic Projects** – Examples: class reports, research projects, design portfolios
- **Professional Projects** – Examples: internships, work assignments, study abroad programs
- **Volunteer or Social Projects** – Examples: organizing a fundraiser, coordinating a group event, community outreach
- **University-Related Projects** – Examples: campus job initiatives, student-produced media, committee service
- **Personal Projects** – Examples: church or community arts programs, neighborhood improvement efforts

Focus especially on projects where you've played an **active or administrative role**—the kind where you might be expected to update a group of stakeholders.

Tip: Before you make your final topic selection, identify your intended audience and the occasion for your speech. This will help you frame the report in a way that feels authentic and realistic.

AUDIENCE IDENTIFICATION AND ANALYSIS

Once you've chosen your project, the next step is figuring out who will care most about your update. These are your **stakeholders**—the individuals or groups who have a direct interest in the project's progress.

In our class presentations, your peers will role-play as your target audience, so you'll need to clearly define who that audience is.

Questions to Guide You
Ask yourself:

- Who has invested time, money, or resources into this project?
- Who will be directly affected by its success or setbacks?
- Who has a vested interest in seeing it completed?

Possible Audiences

- A panel of faculty reviewing your research
- Members of an organization, club, or internship team
- Campus leaders or administrators
- Local residents or community members impacted by your project

Factors to Consider When Analyzing Your Audience
As you read the chapter on audience analysis, pay attention to:

- **Background and demographics** – educational level, profession, cultural background, etc.
- **Reason for interest** – why they care about your project's outcome
- **Attitude toward your project** – are they supportive, skeptical, or opposed?
- **Age and experience level** – how familiar they are with the topic and the work involved

Why This Matters:
A well-defined audience analysis will shape nearly every decision you make about your speech—from what evidence you present to how you organize your ideas, choose your language, and design your visuals.

Occasion

Think about the kind of event or setting where your progress report would be delivered. This context helps determine your tone, formality, and level of detail. Possible occasions might include:

- A regular **organization meeting** where members expect project updates
- A **graduation symposium** highlighting student achievements and initiatives
- A **service learning seminar** focused on community-based work
- A **city council meeting** addressing local government projects or policies

Choosing a realistic occasion will help you make your speech more authentic and relevant to the audience's expectations.

RESEARCH OPTIONS

For this speech, research doesn't have to come exclusively from the library. Think about your own experiences and the people or materials you've encountered while working on your project. Below are possible types of evidence you can use, along with examples of how to format them in **APA** style. Any format style is acceptable—just be consistent.

1. **Expert Testimony**
    - Interview someone with direct knowledge or oversight of your project. This might be your internship supervisor, a construction project manager, your church youth coordinator, or a campus policy-maker.
    - **Tip:** This person should *not* be part of your target audience—they are a resource, not a listener for your speech.
        - **APA Example – Personal Interview:**
            - Smith, J. (2019, March 20). *Personal interview with construction manager.* New York, NY.
2. **Peer Testimony**
    - Include comments from someone who worked alongside you on the project. Use this sparingly—peers may not have full knowledge of the entire project, but they can offer a valuable personal perspective.
        - **APA Example – Peer Interview:**
            - Johnson, M. (2020, April 5). *Personal interview with project teammate.* New York, NY.
3. **Promotional Materials**
    - Use brochures, event programs, or official organizational websites for background information. (Note: Use only *official* sites—not personal blogs or unofficial pages.)
        - **APA Example – Brochure:**

- American Red Cross. (2019, May). *Donating your time to save lives* [Brochure]. Red Cross Headquarters, New York, NY.
  - **APA Example – Organizational Website:**
    - American Red Cross. (2019, May). *Donating your time to save lives.* Retrieved from https://www.redcross.org
4. **Policy or Legal Documents**
   - This could include bylaws, local laws that regulate an event, or university policies that guide your project.
     - **APA Example – Government Document:**
       - City of New York. (2018). *Noise control code* (Title 24, Chapter 2). New York, NY.
5. **Local News Coverage**
   - Newspaper articles can provide context, history, or public reception of your project. Local and campus papers are often the most relevant.
     - **APA Example – Newspaper Article:**
       - Doe, J. (2020, June 15). City council approves new park design. *The New York Times,* pp. A1, A4.
6. **Standard Academic Sources**
   - Books, peer-reviewed journals, and research databases are always valid sources.

MANAGING QUESTIONS AND ANSWERS

Handling audience questions effectively can make your presentation feel polished and confident. Use the strategies from Chapter 24 of our textbook, and plan ahead so your presentation ends with *your* words—not someone else's. Always save a prepared closing line to deliver after the Q&A, ensuring the final takeaway comes from you.

Q&A Protocol

1. **Transition Smoothly into Questions**
   - Briefly restate your main points and thesis before inviting questions. This keeps your key message fresh in the audience's mind.
2. **Repeat or Rephrase Questions**
   - This confirms you understood the question and allows the rest of the audience to hear it clearly. You can also include the topic in your answer to provide context.
3. **Engage with the Entire Audience**
   - Begin by making eye contact with the person who asked the question, then look around the room to include everyone in your response.
4. **Pause Before Answering**

- A short pause helps you gather your thoughts and answer with clarity rather than rushing.
5. **Keep Responses Focused**
    - Be direct—avoid turning your answer into a second speech.
6. **Acknowledge Limits**
    - If you don't know the answer, be honest. Offer to follow up later with more information.
7. **Close with Impact**
    - After answering all questions, deliver your prepared final statement to reinforce your message and leave a strong impression.

PROGRESS REPORT SPEECH – AUDIENCE ANALYSIS

Type and submit as assigned. After deciding on the focus of your progress report, answer the following:

I. Setting
In what type of meeting or gathering would this speech take place?

- An academic committee reviewing your work?
- A monthly meeting for a campus club or organization?
- An update to your employer or supervisor?
- A classroom report on a research project?
- A presentation at a PTA or City Council meeting?

II. Audience Profile
Who would be in the room?
Refer to *Audience Analysis* (Chapter 18). Consider:

- **Disposition** – What do they already know about your project? How do they feel about it—supportive, neutral, or skeptical?
- **Demographics** – Age range, education level, cultural background, professional experience, etc.

III. Audience Connection

- How will you engage and appeal to this audience?
    - Refer to *Chapter 19* for strategies on connecting through shared values, relevant examples, and audience-centered language.

IV. Research Plan

- What kinds of sources will you include?
    - Interviews with key stakeholders
    - Credible websites and reports
    - Articles from databases like CT
- How will this research strengthen your credibility as a speaker? (*See Chapter 26 for guidance on building ethos.*)

PRESENTATION PLAN – KEYWORD OUTLINE – ONGOING PROJECT REPORT

Your outline and bibliography will be graded as part of your *message preparation* process.
MAP:

- **Message:** _____
- **Audience:** _____
- **Purpose:** To inform

Introduction *(Write this section in full sentences)*

- Capture the audience's attention
- Clearly state your purpose and introduce your topic
- Show why the topic matters—connect it to the audience and establish your credibility
- Present a thesis statement with a preview of your main points

Transition to the first main point
Body *(Keyword Outline)*
I. Project Background – Explain the project's purpose and give any background information your chosen audience will need to understand it.

- A.
  - 1.
  - 2.
- B.
  - 1.
  - 2.

(Transition – fully written out)

II. Work Completed – Describe the work that has been finished so far. Compare it to the original plan. Note any unexpected challenges, delays, or costs.

- A.
  - 1.
  - 2.
- B.
  - 1.
  - 2.

(Transition – fully written out)

III. Current Status – Explain what is happening now. Include any changes that have been made to your plan or process and why.

- A.
  - 1.
  - 2.
- B.
  - 1.
  - 2.

(Transition – fully written out)
IV. Remaining Work – Identify the steps left to finish the project. Discuss your goals, expectations, and any plan revisions. Indicate whether the original deadline is still realistic and explain your reasoning.

- A.
  - 1.
  - 2.
- B.
  - 1.
  - 2.

(Transition)
Conclusion *(Write this section in full sentences)*

- Evaluate the project's overall effectiveness
- Summarize major accomplishments or offer cautions
- Avoid introducing new ideas here
- Invite questions from the audience
- Deliver a final closing statement once Q&A is over

Note: You may include a short bibliography at the end of your outline instead of on a separate page.

PRESENTATION PLAN – KEYWORD OUTLINE – COMPLETED PROJECT REPORT

Your outline and bibliography will be graded as part of your *message preparation* process.
MAP:

- **Message:** _____
- **Audience:** _____
- **Purpose:** To inform

Introduction *(Write this section in full sentences)*

- Capture the audience's attention
- Clearly state your purpose and introduce your topic
- Show why the topic matters—connect it to the audience and establish your credibility
- Present a thesis statement with a preview of your main points

Transition to the first main point
Body *(Keyword Outline)*
I. Project Background – Explain the project's purpose and give any background information your chosen audience will need to understand it.

- A.
  - 1.
  - 2.
- B.
  - 1.
  - 2.

(Transition – fully written out)

II. Work Completed – Describe the work that has been finished so far. Compare it to the original plan. Note any unexpected challenges, delays, or costs.

- A.
  - 1.
  - 2.
- B.
  - 1.
  - 2.

(Transition – fully written out)

III. Problem/Solution – Were there any hiccups during your project? What was done to address it?

- A.
  - 1.
  - 2.
- B.
  - 1.
  - 2.

(Transition – fully written out)
IV. Future Recommendations – What would you recommend to someone else completing a similar project? Are there any key takeaways? Words of advice? Be specific!

- A.
  - 1.
  - 2.
- B.
  - 1.
  - 2.

(Transition)
Conclusion *(Write this section in full sentences)*

- Evaluate the project's overall effectiveness
- Summarize major accomplishments or offer cautions
- Avoid introducing new ideas here
- Invite questions from the audience
- Deliver a final closing statement once Q&A is over

Note: You may include a short bibliography at the end of your outline instead of on a separate page.

Progress Report – Critique Form   Speaker _____

Missing, Ineffective, Satisfactory, Good, Excellent **Notes**

Competencies	Part I: Message Preparation – Appropriate for speaker, topic, audience, occasion, and purpose	M	I	S	G	E
Topic	Chooses and narrows topic; Meets general purpose					
	*Careful connection with audience needs/interests					
Support/ Organization	Uses a chronological organization pattern					
	Intro – Uses attention-getter; identifies topic & purpose; establishes relevance & credibility; previews main points; transitions to 1st main point					
	***Body** -- Provides appropriate supporting material with vivid and specific details (Background; Work completed; Present status; Work remaining)					
	Use of transitions within the speech					
	Presentation aid -- Design of effective PowerPoint					
	***Conclusion** – Review of key points; memorable thought stated after Q&A					
Q&A	* **Effective management of Q&A** (Restated/rephrased question)					
	Part I: Overall					
	Part II Energetic Message Delivery – Appropriate for audience, occasion, and purpose	M	I	S	G	E
Language	*Uses appropriate language for the designated audience and connects it to the audience					
	*Effective oral citation of sources C1 C2					
Voice	**Variety** – Uses vocal variety in volume, rate, pitch & intensity to heighten and maintain interest.					
	Accuracy – Uses pronunciation, grammar, & articulation; minimizes filler words.					
Physical Behaviors	**Manner, movement and gestures** – Uses movement and gestures effectively; no roots or fidgeting					
	***Eye contact and Facial expression** – Uses facial expressiveness and eye contact to support the message and engage with listeners					
	Notes – Effectively uses appropriately designed notes to support speech					
	***Presentation aid** – Effectively presents Power-Point to enhance speech (not repeat message)					
Time?	*Part II: Overall*					

*Focal points for this speech – addressed in the reading and homework for this unit

Strengths? Areas for improvement?   Critiqued by _____

TALK LIKE YOU MEAN IT   59

Progress Report – Critique Form   **Speaker** _____

Missing, Ineffective, Satisfactory, Good, Excellent *Notes*

Competencies	Part I: Message Preparation – Appropriate for speaker, topic, audience, occasion, and purpose	M	I	S	G	E
Topic	Chooses and narrows topic; Meets general purpose					
	*Careful connection with audience needs/interests					
Support/ Organization	Uses a chronological organization pattern					
	Intro – Uses attention-getter; identifies topic & purpose; establishes relevance & credibility; previews main points; transitions to 1st main point					
	***Body** -- Provides appropriate supporting material with vivid and specific details (Background; Work completed; Present status; Work remaining)					
	Use of transitions within the speech					
	Presentation aid -- Design of effective PowerPoint					
	***Conclusion** – Review of key points; memorable thought stated after Q&A					
Q&A	* **Effective management of Q&A** (Restated/rephrased question)					
	Part I: Overall					
	Part II Energetic Message Delivery – Appropriate for audience, occasion, and purpose	M	I	S	G	E
Language	*Uses appropriate language for the designated audience and connects it to the audience					
	*Effective oral citation of sources C1 C2					
Voice	**Variety** – Uses vocal variety in volume, rate, pitch & intensity to heighten and maintain interest.					
	Accuracy – Uses pronunciation, grammar, & articulation; minimizes filler words.					
Physical Behaviors	**Manner, movement and gestures** – Uses movement and gestures effectively; no roots or fidgeting					
	***Eye contact and Facial expression** – Uses facial expressiveness and eye contact to support the message and engage with listeners					
	Notes – Effectively uses appropriately designed notes to support speech					
	***Presentation aid** – Effectively presents Power-Point to enhance speech (not repeat message)					
Time?	*Part II: Overall*					

*Focal points for this speech – addressed in the reading and homework for this unit

Strengths? Areas for improvement?   *Critiqued by* _____

LINCOLN COSTELLO

Progress Report – Critique Form   Speaker _____

Missing, Ineffective, Satisfactory, Good, Excellent *Notes*

Competencies	Part I: Message Preparation – Appropriate for speaker, topic, audience, occasion, and purpose	M	I	S	G	E
Topic	Chooses and narrows topic; Meets general purpose					
	*Careful connection with audience needs/interests					
Support/ Organization	Uses a chronological organization pattern					
	Intro – Uses attention-getter; identifies topic & purpose; establishes relevance & credibility; previews main points; transitions to 1st main point					
	***Body** -- Provides appropriate supporting material with vivid and specific details (Background; Work completed; Present status; Work remaining)					
	Use of transitions within the speech					
	Presentation aid -- Design of effective PowerPoint					
	***Conclusion** – Review of key points; memorable thought stated after Q&A					
Q&A	* **Effective management of Q&A** (Restated/rephrased question)					
	Part I: Overall					
	*Part II **Energetic** Message Delivery – Appropriate for audience, occasion, and purpose*	M	I	S	G	E
Language	*Uses appropriate language for the designated audience and connects it to the audience					
	*Effective oral citation of sources C1 C2					
Voice	**Variety** – Uses vocal variety in volume, rate, pitch & intensity to heighten and maintain interest.					
	Accuracy – Uses pronunciation, grammar, & articulation; minimizes filler words.					
Physical Behaviors	**Manner, movement and gestures** – Uses movement and gestures effectively; no roots or fidgeting					
	***Eye contact and Facial expression** – Uses facial expressiveness and eye contact to support the message and engage with listeners					
	Notes – Effectively uses appropriately designed notes to support speech					
	***Presentation aid** – Effectively presents Power-Point to enhance speech (not repeat message)					
Time?	*Part II: Overall*					

*Focal points for this speech – addressed in the reading and homework for this unit

Strengths? Areas for improvement?   Critiqued by _____

CHAPTER 4
ISSUE ANALYSIS

1. Required Readings	*Course Handbook* – Unit IV
	Ch. 25 – Understanding Argumentation
	Ch. 26 – Building Evidence
	Ch. 27 – Presentation Aids Pt. 3: Advanced Media
	Ch. 28 – Delivering Persuasive Speeches
	Sample Speeches – BrightSpace
2. Quizzes	*Course Guide*, Chapters 25–28, sample speeches
3. Participation Points	Online and in-class activities; Midterm; REAL PS 4
4. Speech Assignment	Issue Analysis

ISSUE ANALYSIS FOCUS AREAS:

- **Research** – Gather information from credible sources to understand the viewpoints on an issue.
- **Ethics** – Develop your argument with integrity, presenting all sides fairly without omission.
- **Analysis** – Examine the context of the issue, considering the setting, audience, and occasion in which it will be discussed.
- **Language & Listening** – Use language that fosters clarity and mutual understanding rather than triggering emotional reactions. Practice active listening so you can identify well-reasoned arguments and respond accurately.

When you're tasked with explaining two or more perspectives on a single issue, you face a unique challenge: your goal is to inform, not persuade. This requires maintaining a high level of ethical responsibility—keeping personal opinions out of your delivery and ensuring your presentation is balanced. A successful informative speaker approaches the task as a facilitator of understanding, helping the audience see the full landscape of the issue without being pushed toward one conclusion.

SPEECH 4 - PRESENTING AN ISSUE ANALYSIS

This assignment gives you the opportunity to choose a current controversy and present it to an audience that may need clear, unbiased information about the topic.

In both your personal and professional life, you will encounter disagreements, complex problems, and opposing viewpoints that can stand in the way of your goals. You may already have strong feelings about certain issues and a clear sense of what you believe should be done. It's natural to want others to see the matter from your perspective.

However, before you can effectively advocate for change or persuade anyone, it is essential to first research the issue thoroughly and understand it from multiple viewpoints. Professionals are often called upon to investigate all sides of a problem so they can help their organization, clients, or community make informed decisions.

By using a variety of credible sources—including FIT's library databases—you will gain a broad, balanced understanding of the controversy. In this speech, avoid focusing only on information that supports your personal stance. Instead, present each side fairly, the way a journalist might objectively report on two opposing groups at a protest. Even if the reporter privately supports one group, their final article must remain neutral.

Similarly, you might be asked to represent opposing student opinions on a campus issue, such as new construction plans. In that case, your role is not to choose sides but to present each position accurately and objectively. The goal is to inform your audience—not persuade them.

ISSUE ANALYSIS SPEECH GUIDELINES

Your fourth formal speech builds on the skills from Speeches 1–3, increasing complexity and challenging you to address a controversial issue with balance and depth. Rather than persuading, your role is to inform your audience about multiple perspectives on the issue so they can form their own conclusions.

Step 1: Understanding the Assignment

- **Type:** Issue analysis, delivered extemporaneously (planned in advance but not read word-for-word).
- **Level of Difficulty:** Level 4 — includes all skills from Levels 1–3, plus advanced research, structure, and balanced viewpoint presentation.
- **Purpose:** To inform your audience about a controversy while avoiding a one-sided, biased delivery.
- **Audience:** Stakeholders who need accurate, balanced information about the controversy.

Step 2: Choosing and Focusing Your Topic
Your topic should:

- Be controversial and connected to your interests, involvement, or academic major.
- Matter to your audience and have real-world implications.
- Be narrow enough to explain in detail within the time limit.

Step 3: Building Credibility
You will be expected to:

- Use personal interest or experience to connect with your audience.
- Select credible, balanced sources to represent multiple perspectives.
- Cite a minimum of **4 sources** from varied types (including library databases).
- Provide **both** a written bibliography and **oral citations** during the speech.

Note: Insufficient oral citation will result in a point deduction.

· · ·

Step 4: Organizing Your Speech
Choose one of the following structures:

- Compare–Contrast
- Cause–Effect
- Problem–Solution
- Topical

Ensure your organization:

- Opens with a clear introduction.
- Presents balanced perspectives logically.
- Closes with a memorable conclusion.

Step 5: Voice, Language, and Delivery
Speak with appropriate vocal variety to hold attention.

- Use language suited to your audience and free from loaded or biased terms.
- Integrate a variety of physical strategies (eye contact, gestures, posture) while mastering your use of technology.

Step 6: Presentation Aids
Use **4–6 PowerPoint slides** plus spacer slides (advanced technique).

- Avoid overloading slides with text — let visuals support your words.

Step 7: Time & Notes

- **Length:** 6 ½ – 7 ½ minutes.
- **Notes:** Minimal keyword notes only — do not read from a script.

Why This Speech Matters

This assignment will sharpen your ability to:

- Communicate complex, divisive issues with fairness and clarity.
- Balance thorough research with audience-friendly delivery.
- Use structure, language, and delivery strategies to maintain credibility in professional and academic contexts.

SPEECH PREPARATION AND DELIVERY

To deliver an effective presentation, you'll move through the following stages:

1. Invention

- **Select a relevant topic.** Consider issues or debates connected to your campus (e.g., dining services, online learning), your academic field, or your home or local community. Choose something you already have some familiarity with and genuine interest in exploring further.
- **Define your speaking context** and create a preliminary MAP (Message, Audience, Purpose).
- **Identify audience needs** so you can tailor your content and delivery.
- **Gather supporting material** from a range of sources, including your own prior knowledge, credible library database research, and—if applicable—primary sources such as interviews or surveys.

2. Arrangement

- **Choose a logical structure** for your speech. Possible organizational patterns include:
  - Topical
  - Cause–effect
  - Problem–solution
- **Develop a presentation plan** that outlines your key points, transitions, and flow.

3. Style

- Use **language** that suits your specific audience's background and expectations.
- Provide **details** that are relevant and clear for your listeners' level of knowledge.

4. Memory and Delivery

- **Design and prepare at least four PowerPoint slides**, including at least one example of simple animation.
- **Rehearse multiple times** to refine timing, flow, and confidence.
- **Present using minimal notes**, ideally a keyword outline rather than a full script.

Related Writing Tasks

- Prepare and submit your **presentation plan**, **context analysis**, and **bibliography**.
- Complete **peer critiques** to give constructive feedback on classmates' speeches.

TOPIC POSSIBILITIES – ISSUE ANALYSIS: PRESENTING MULTIPLE PERSPECTIVES

When selecting a topic for your issue analysis, aim for a controversy that you already understand well and feel passionate about—something that will engage both you and your audience. Choose a subject that is timely, relevant, and manageable in scope. Avoid topics that are overused or overly complex for this assignment (such as gun control, abortion, marijuana legalization, or stem cell research). Your familiarity with the topic and genuine enthusiasm will help create a stronger, more credible presentation.

Brainstorming Your Topic

To generate ideas, start with a list of at least ten possible topics. Use the prompts below to guide your brainstorming:

1. **Campus Issues (2–3 topics)**
   - Recent or proposed policy changes
   - New building projects or renovations
   - Tuition or fee adjustments
2. **Local Community Issues (2–3 topics)**
   - Controversies affecting your town or housing complex

- Neighborhood disputes or community improvement projects
3. **Academic Field Controversies (2–3 topics)**
    - Theoretical debates within your major
    - Competing solutions for a recurring problem in your field
4. **Hometown Concerns (2–3 topics)**
    - Proposed construction projects, such as a shopping center
    - Zoning law changes or neighborhood development disputes
5. **Local or State Political Topics (2–3 topics)**
    - Policy proposals in city or state government
    - Recent legislative changes affecting your community

Finalizing Your Selection

Before choosing your final topic:

- Ensure the controversy is **current and relevant**.
- Confirm that you can present **two or more distinct perspectives** on the issue.
- Consider whether your topic lends itself to objective analysis rather than persuasion.
- Refer to the **Context Analysis** section (Handbook p. 71) to evaluate fit for the assignment.

IDENTIFYING YOUR AUDIENCE OF STAKEHOLDERS

Once you have selected your topic, determine the specific groups or individuals who have a vested interest in the issue. These stakeholders will shape your approach—impacting what research you gather, how you organize your points, the examples you choose, and the tone or style of language you use.

For instance, if your topic focuses on changes to FIT tuition, possible audiences could include:

- College administrators
- Prospective or current students
- Parents and families of students
- Alumni
- Local or state legislators

Your speech will be most effective when tailored to a **single, clearly defined audience**. By analyzing that group's needs, existing knowledge, and concerns, you can deliver information in a way that resonates and holds credibility.

. . .

Research Strategies for Your Chosen Audience

- **Use credible sources.** Start with FIT's library databases to gather reliable, well-vetted information. Avoid crowd-sourced resources like Wikipedia.
- **Diversify your research.** Depending on your audience, consult government publications, reputable news outlets, industry reports, or scholarly journals.
- **Match the source to the listener.** For a scholarly audience, prioritize peer-reviewed journal articles. For policymakers, government reports or economic impact studies may be more persuasive. For the general public, look for clear, accessible magazine or newspaper articles.
- **Evaluate credibility.** Ask yourself: *Will this source be respected by my audience? Does it meet their standards for accuracy and reliability?*

For additional guidance on source evaluation and research methods, refer to the resources provided on your course's Brightspace site.

ISSUE ANALYSIS SPEECH – CONTEXT ANALYSIS

Complete this form before drafting your presentation plan. Your responses will help you—and your instructor—understand the setting, audience, and purpose for your speech.

    MAP:

- **Message:** *(Briefly summarize the central focus of your speech.)*
- **Audience:** *(Who will be listening? Define them specifically.)*
- **Purpose:** To inform **[insert audience description]** about **[insert topic]**.

Speech Occasion

Describe the setting or event where this speech would be delivered.
Examples:

- Town hall meeting in your neighborhood
- Shareholder or committee meeting
- Academic conference
- PTA meeting
- Monthly gathering of a nonprofit
- Social club meeting

Speaker–Listener Relationship

Your expertise on the issue: *(What personal, academic, or professional knowledge do you bring to the topic?)*

Choose one that best describes your audience's expertise:

- Audience members have a general understanding of the field, but you hold deeper knowledge about this specific issue. *(Example: presenting a senior thesis to faculty.)*
- Audience members share a similar general background to yours, but you have done more research or have unique insights. *(Example: updating co-workers on a new project.)*
- Audience members are interested but have little to no prior knowledge about the topic. *(Example: speaking to community members about proposed road construction.)*

Audience Analysis
Disposition:

- Toward the topic:
- Toward the speaker:
- Toward the occasion:

Demographics:

- Age range
- Gender breakdown
- Ethnic or cultural background
- Socioeconomic factors
- Religious or political considerations (if relevant)

Setting Considerations

- Physical location and room layout
- Time of day
- Equipment availability (e.g., microphones, screens)

Adapting to Context
Use course references to help guide your preparation:

- **Narrowing the topic:** *(See Chapter 10)*
- **Thesis statement development:** *(See Chapter 12)*
- **Audience demographics and adaptation:** *(See Chapter 18)*

CONSIDERING ORGANIZATION

Because this assignment focuses on presenting multiple perspectives, its structure can be more complex than earlier speeches you've given. In your course text, you'll find several common patterns for organizing a speech—such as **cause-effect**, **problem-solution**, and **topical**—that can help guide you.

Once you have clearly identified your audience and completed your research, you'll decide which organizational pattern best suits your **Multiple Audience Perspectives (MAP)** speech.

No single format works for every situation, so it's important to adapt the structure to your specific topic and audience. However, regardless of the format you choose, keep in mind the underlying **comparison–contrast** framework. Your goal is to present two sides of an issue so that listeners can easily identify both similarities and differences.

Avoid jumping between unrelated categories or comparing mismatched elements ("apples to oranges"). Instead, ensure that both perspectives are examined using the same categories ("apples to apples"). Two common methods for accomplishing this are the **point method** and the **block method**.

TOPICAL ORGANIZATION EXAMPLES

Point Method

In this method, each main point represents a category, and both perspectives are addressed within that same category before moving to the next.

Example: Comparing beliefs about Bigfoot and the Loch Ness Monster
Introduction

1. **Habitat**
    - A. Bigfoot sightings and wilderness locations
    - B. Loch Ness Monster sightings in the Scottish Highlands
2. **Evidence**
    - A. Footprint casts, blurry photographs, eyewitness reports for Bigfoot
    - B. Sonar readings, old photographs, eyewitness reports for Loch Ness
3. **Public Perception**
    - A. How Bigfoot is viewed in North American pop culture
    - B. How the Loch Ness Monster is viewed in Scottish and global folklore

Conclusion

Block Method

In this method, you present all information about one perspective before moving to the other.

Example: Comparing beliefs about Bigfoot and the Loch Ness Monster
Introduction

1. **Bigfoot**
    - A. Habitat and reported locations
    - B. Evidence and key sightings
    - C. Cultural impact and media portrayals
2. **Loch Ness Monster**
    - A. Habitat and reported locations
    - B. Evidence and key sightings
    - C. Cultural impact and media portrayals

Conclusion

BUILDING AN ARGUMENT

When presenting multiple perspectives, each side should have a clear, logical argument. This means structuring your explanation so that your audience can easily follow the reasoning. A strong argument typically includes three components:

1. **Claim** – The main statement or belief being presented.
2. **Evidence/Data** – The facts, examples, or observations that support the claim.
3. **Warrant** – The reasoning that connects the evidence to the claim, explaining why the evidence proves the point.

For example, if you're comparing two lighthearted conspiracies—say, **Bigfoot** and **the Loch Ness Monster**—you would identify what each group of believers claims is true, what evidence they present, and how they connect that evidence to their claim.
Example:

- **Bigfoot Claim:** Large, ape-like creatures roam the forests of North America.
- **Evidence:** Footprint casts, blurry photos, eyewitness accounts.
- **Warrant:** Such evidence is consistent with a living, unidentified primate species.

Example:

- **Loch Ness Claim:** A large aquatic creature lives in Loch Ness, Scotland.
- **Evidence:** Sonar readings, decades of photographs, local folklore.
- **Warrant:** These data points match what one might expect from a surviving prehistoric creature in a deep freshwater environment.

When you explain each side, focus on **accuracy and fairness**—your job here is not to persuade, but to present each argument as clearly and credibly as possible. Avoid emotionally charged or combative language. Instead, let the logic and structure of each side's reasoning speak for itself.

PRESENTATION PLAN – KEYWORD OUTLINE – ISSUE ANALYSIS

Your presentation plan will be reviewed as part of your overall **message preparation**, along with your bibliography and context analysis. Use the **point method** or **block method** outlined earlier to guide the structure of your talk.

MAP:

My goal for this speech based on feedback from previous speeches:

(Write your goal here — for example, to improve transitions, strengthen audience connection, or better balance each perspective.)

Introduction

(Write this section in full sentences — no notes or shorthand.)

- **Attention-Getter:** Open with a surprising fact, short story, or question that hooks the audience.
- **Topic & Purpose:** Clearly introduce the issue and explain why you're presenting it.
- **Motivation – Credibility & Relevance:** Briefly share your connection to the topic and why it matters to your listeners.
- **Thesis & Preview:** State your thesis and outline the main points you'll cover.
- **Transition to First Main Point:** Write this out completely so it flows naturally from your introduction.

Body (Keyword Outline)

- **Organizational Pattern:** Choose whether to use the **point method** or **block method**.
- **Arguments for Each Perspective:** For every viewpoint, identify the **claim**, provide supporting **evidence**, and explain the **warrant** (how the evidence supports the claim).
- **Use a Consistent Format:** Maintain parallel structure when presenting each perspective so your audience can compare easily.
- **Sources:** Show where you'll cite each source.
- **Transition to Conclusion:** Write out your final transition in full.

Conclusion

(Write this section in full sentences — no notes or shorthand.)

- Use a clear signal that the speech is ending, but avoid saying "In conclusion."
- Summarize your main points and restate your topic and purpose.
- Leave the audience with a challenge, call to action, or lasting thought.

Bibliography

Prepare a bibliography using a standard citation style (**APA, Chicago, or MLA**).

Issue Analysis – Peer Critique Form   Speaker _____

Missing, Ineffective, Satisfactory, Good, Excellent *Notes*

Competencies	Part I: Message Preparation – *Appropriate for speaker, topic, audience, occasion, and purpose*	M	I	S	G	E
Topic	Chooses and narrows a topic					
	Meets general purpose – to inform					
Support/ Organization	**Intro** – Uses attention-getter; identifies topic & purpose; establishes relevance & credibility; previews main points; transitions to 1st main point					
	*****Body** – Chooses supporting material to *balance* **each** perspective *equally*					
	*Ethically and objectively *constructs argument(s)* for **each** perspective (claim, data, warrant)					
	*Uses appropriate comparison/contrast organization & transitions (point or block method)					
	*****Presentation aid** – appropriate design of **advanced** PowerPoint (not simply repeat message)					
	Conclusion – Restatement of thesis; concludes with memorable thought					
	Part I: Overall					
	Part II <u>*Energetic*</u> *Message Delivery – Appropriate for audience, occasion, and purpose*	M	I	S	G	E
Language	*Uses appropriate language for the designated audience and context					
	Effective oral citation of scholarly sources C1 C2 C3 C4					
Voice	**Variety** – Uses vocal variety in volume, rate, pitch & intensity to heighten and maintain interest.					
	*****Accuracy** – Uses pronunciation, grammar, & articulation; minimizes filler words.					
Physical Behaviors	*****Manner, movement, gestures** – Uses movement and gestures effectively; no roots or t-rex arms.					
	*****Eye contact and Facial expression** – Uses facial expressiveness and eye contact to support the message and engage with listeners					
	Notes – Effectively uses appropriately designed notes to support speech					
	*****Presentation aid** -- Effectively presents **advanced** PowerPoint to enhance speech					
Time?	**Part II: Overall**					

* Focal points for this speech – addressed in reading and homework

Notes

Critiqued by _____

LINCOLN COSTELLO

Issue Analysis – Peer Critique Form   Speaker _____

Missing, Ineffective, Satisfactory, Good, Excellent ***Notes***

Competencies	*Part I: Message Preparation – Appropriate for speaker, topic, audience, occasion, and purpose*	M	I	S	G	E
Topic	Chooses and narrows a topic					
	Meets general purpose – to inform					
Support/ Organization	**Intro** – Uses attention-getter; identifies topic & purpose; establishes relevance & credibility; previews main points; transitions to 1st main point					
	*****Body** – Chooses supporting material to *balance* **each** perspective *equally*					
	*Ethically and objectively *constructs argument(s)* for **each** perspective (claim, data, warrant)					
	*Uses appropriate comparison/contrast organization & transitions (point or block method)					
	*****Presentation aid** – appropriate design of **advanced** PowerPoint (not simply repeat message)					
	Conclusion – Restatement of thesis; concludes with memorable thought					
	Part I: Overall					
	*Part II **Energetic** Message Delivery – Appropriate for audience, occasion, and purpose*	M	I	S	G	E
Language	*Uses appropriate language for the designated audience and context					
	Effective oral citation of scholarly sources **C1 C2 C3 C4**					
Voice	**Variety** – Uses vocal variety in volume, rate, pitch & intensity to heighten and maintain interest.					
	*****Accuracy** – Uses pronunciation, grammar, & articulation; minimizes filler words.					
Physical Behaviors	*****Manner, movement, gestures** – Uses movement and gestures effectively; no roots or t-rex arms.					
	*****Eye contact and Facial expression** – Uses facial expressiveness and eye contact to support the message and engage with listeners					
	Notes – Effectively uses appropriately designed notes to support speech					
	*****Presentation aid** -- Effectively presents **advanced** PowerPoint to enhance speech					
Time?	***Part II: Overall***					

* *Focal points for this speech – addressed in reading and homework*

Notes

Critiqued by _____

Issue Analysis – Peer Critique Form   Speaker _____

Missing, Ineffective, Satisfactory, Good, Excellent *Notes*

Competencies	Part I: Message Preparation – *Appropriate for speaker, topic, audience, occasion, and purpose*	M	I	S	G	E
Topic	Chooses and narrows a topic					
	Meets general purpose – to inform					
Support/ Organization	**Intro** – Uses attention-getter; identifies topic & purpose; establishes relevance & credibility; previews main points; transitions to 1st main point					
	***Body** – Chooses supporting material to *balance* **each** perspective *equally*					
	*Ethically and objectively *constructs argument(s)* for **each** perspective (claim, data, warrant)					
	*Uses appropriate comparison/contrast organization & transitions (point or block method)					
	***Presentation aid** – appropriate design of **advanced** PowerPoint (not simply repeat message)					
	Conclusion – Restatement of thesis; concludes with memorable thought					
	Part I: Overall					
	Part II <u>Energetic</u> *Message Delivery – Appropriate for audience, occasion, and purpose*	M	I	S	G	E
Language	*Uses appropriate language for the designated audience and context					
	Effective oral citation of scholarly sources C1 C2 C3 C4					
Voice	**Variety** – Uses vocal variety in volume, rate, pitch & intensity to heighten and maintain interest.					
	***Accuracy** – Uses pronunciation, grammar, & articulation; minimizes filler words.					
Physical Behaviors	***Manner, movement, gestures** – Uses movement and gestures effectively; no roots or t-rex arms.					
	***Eye contact and Facial expression** – Uses facial expressiveness and eye contact to support the message and engage with listeners					
	Notes – Effectively uses appropriately designed notes to support speech					
	***Presentation aid** -- Effectively presents **advanced** PowerPoint to enhance speech					
Time?	*Part II: Overall*					

* *Focal points for this speech – addressed in reading and homework*

Notes

Critiqued by _____

CHAPTER 5
PERSUASIVE SPEECH

1. Required Readings	*Course Handbook* – Unit V
	Ch. 29 – Organizing for Persuasion
	Ch. 30 – Presenting in Groups
	Ch. 31 – Speaking for Special Occasions
	Ch. 32 – Presentations in Other College Courses
	Sample Speeches – BrightSpace
2. Quizzes	*Course Guide*, Chapters 29–32, sample speeches
3. Participation Points	Online and in-class activities; PRPSA; REAL PS 5
4. Speech Assignment	Persuasive Speech

PERSUASIVE SPEECH FOCAL AREAS:

- **Research** – Investigate your topic thoroughly to understand multiple sides of the argument.
- **Ethics** – Use emotional appeals responsibly and avoid manipulative tactics.
- **Analysis** – Consider the setting, audience, and occasion before shaping your message.
- **Language & Listening** – Choose persuasive language that resonates with your audience, and practice active listening to identify strong, logical points.

A persuasive speech aims to influence the audience's attitudes, beliefs, or values, guiding them toward the speaker's perspective. To do this effectively, a presenter must balance logic, credibility, and emotion—without resorting to unethical or exaggerated claims.

For this assignment, the emphasis is on **crafting a compelling delivery**. While credible evidence is still essential, the research portion is streamlined so you can focus on structuring your arguments, engaging the audience, and refining your persuasive techniques. Because of this, this speech carries slightly less weight than other major speaking assignments.

SPEECH 5 – DELIVERING THE PERSUASIVE SPEECH

This assignment gives you the opportunity to choose a topic you care about, research it thoroughly, and present it in a way that motivates your audience to see it from your perspective. Your listeners may already have some opinions or assumptions about the topic—or they may know very little about it—so your job is to provide clear, credible, and convincing information that moves them toward your viewpoint.

Effective persuasive speeches combine **logos** (logical reasoning), **pathos** (emotional appeal), and **ethos** (speaker credibility). Using these rhetorical proofs in balance will make your speech far more compelling than relying on any single approach. This means you'll need to:

- **Build trust** with your audience through your credibility and preparedness.
- **Support your claims** with solid evidence from credible sources.
- **Connect emotionally** by showing your audience why the topic matters to them.

Persuasive speaking is one of the most valuable communication skills you can develop. You'll use it in job interviews, team meetings, negotiations, community advocacy, and even everyday conversations. This speech is your chance to practice the kind of persuasive communication that will serve you throughout your professional and personal life.

PERSUASIVE SPEECH GUIDELINES

Your fifth formal speech builds on the skills from Speeches 1–4, adding persuasive techniques and more advanced delivery strategies. This time, you'll not only inform — you'll aim to influence your audience's beliefs or actions.

Step 1: Understanding the Assignment

- **Type:** Persuasive speech, delivered extemporaneously (planned in advance but not read word-for-word).
- **Level of Difficulty:** Level 5 — incorporates all skills from previous speeches (Levels 1–4) and adds persuasive strategy and audience engagement.
- **Purpose:** To convince your audience to adopt your point of view or take a specific action.
- **Audience:** Stakeholders, decision-makers, or peers who could be directly affected by your topic.

Step 2: Choosing and Focusing Your Topic
Your topic should:

- Address a controversial issue or propose a new invention/solution.
- Be connected to your own knowledge, experience, or interests.
- Be narrow enough to make a persuasive case in just a few minutes.

Step 3: Building Credibility
You will be expected to:

- Combine personal expertise with authoritative sources.
- Select details ethically to present an accurate and fair picture of your case.
- Analyze your audience and adapt your approach for maximum impact.

Step 4: Organizing Your Speech

- Use **Monroe's Motivated Sequence** to structure your argument.

- Open with a compelling hook to gain attention.
- Clearly state your call to action.
- Use transitions to guide your audience through each step of your case.

Step 5: Voice, Language, and Delivery

- Speak with persuasive language and varied vocal tone.
- Match your word choice to your audience's values and priorities.
- Integrate confident physical delivery (eye contact, gestures, posture).
- Demonstrate mastery of any technology used in your presentation.

Step 6: Presentation Aids

- Use 1–2 PowerPoint slides (plus spacer slides if needed).
- Keep slides simple — use images, minimal text, and clean design.
- Ensure visuals reinforce your message rather than distract from it.

Step 7: Time & Confidence

- **Length:** 2–3 minutes.
- **Confidence:** Treat this as a professional pitch — rehearse until your delivery feels natural and persuasive.

Why This Speech Matters

This assignment challenges you to apply all your prior public speaking skills in a persuasive context. You'll be practicing:

- Crafting arguments that move people to action.
- Balancing emotional appeal with factual support.
- Using structure and delivery to inspire confidence and credibility.

SPEECH PREPARATION AND DELIVERY

To deliver a successful persuasive presentation, follow these key steps from start to finish:

1. Invention

- **Select a relevant topic** – Choose something timely and meaningful. This could be a campus debate, a local issue in New York City, or a topic that impacts college students more broadly.
- **Draft a preliminary MAP** – Outline your *Main Argument Plan* to guide you.
- **Analyze your audience** – Understand their needs, interests, and potential biases.
- **Gather evidence** – Use a mix of personal experience, prior knowledge, and credible research. Pull from library databases, reputable online sources, and, if applicable, primary research such as interviews or surveys.

2. Arrangement

- **Organize using Monroe's Motivated Sequence** – This five-step pattern (Attention, Need, Satisfaction, Visualization, Action) is highly effective for persuasion.
- **Develop a presentation plan** – Decide how each part of your argument will flow and how you'll connect the sections smoothly.

3. Style

- **Adapt your language to your audience** – Choose persuasive wording that resonates without alienating.
- **Include appropriate detail** – Provide enough explanation and examples to be convincing without overwhelming the listener.

4. Memory & Delivery

- **Design engaging visuals** – Create 1–2 slides with tasteful animations. Use spacer slides to give the audience moments to focus on your words rather than the screen.

- **Rehearse thoroughly** – Practice with your visuals and notes until your delivery feels natural.
- **Present confidently** – Use notes as prompts, not a script, to maintain eye contact and connection with your audience.

Related Writing Assignments

- **Presentation plan and bibliography** – Include sources in a consistent citation style (APA, MLA, or Chicago).
- **Peer critiques** – Offer constructive feedback on classmates' speeches, focusing on both strengths and areas for improvement.

TOPIC POSSIBILITIES – PERSUASIVE SPEECH

When selecting a persuasive speech topic, choose an issue you genuinely care about and already have some knowledge of. Passion for your subject will make your research and delivery stronger.

Brainstorming Prompts

Create a list of at least ten possible topics. Use the following categories to guide your ideas:

- **2–3 New or Improved Products**
    - Examples: An app that simplifies campus meal planning, a foldable bike for city commuters, or a reusable coffee cup with built-in temperature control.
- **2–3 Controversies in New York City**
    - Examples: Expansion of bike lanes, rent control debates, or the impact of late-night subway service changes.
- **2–3 Controversies Affecting College Students**
    - Examples: Rising tuition costs, textbook affordability, or the role of AI in coursework.
- **2–3 Campus Resources Worth Promoting**
    - Examples: Writing center services, mental health counseling, or career services workshops.
- **2–3 Campus Controversies**
    - Examples: Space allocation for student clubs, sustainability practices on campus, or student government policies.

Audience of Stakeholders

Once you've chosen your topic, list the groups or individuals who have a vested interest in the issue. Then, select one target audience and perform an audience analysis. Consider:

- Their level of knowledge about the topic.
- Their values, needs, and concerns.
- What kind of evidence will resonate with them.

Your findings will shape your main points, examples, tone, and structure.

Research Possibilities

Use credible library databases to fill in gaps in your knowledge. Combine this research with your own experiences or observations for a well-rounded perspective. Remember to cite your sources in the format you're using for the course (APA, MLA, or Chicago). You can also incorporate research methods from earlier assignments—such as surveys, interviews, or field observations—to add unique evidence.

PRESENTATION PLAN – KEYWORD OUTLINE – PERSUASIVE SPEECH

Use this model as a reference when creating your typed keyword outline.

Note: This is **not** a full-sentence draft — keep it concise. Your instructor will review this plan as part of your **message preparation** grade.

MAP

- **Message:** _____
- **Audience:** _____
- **Purpose:** To persuade

Introduction *(Write this section in full sentences)*

- **Attention-getter:** _____
- **Why it matters (Relevance):** _____
- **Thesis:** *(Set the tone and focus without revealing every detail)*
- **Transition to First Main Point:** *(Write the complete transition sentence here)*

Body *(Keyword Format)*
I. Need (First Main Point)

- Present the challenge, problem, or situation.
- Use vivid details and sensory description.
- **Transition:** _____

II. Satisfaction (Second Main Point)

- Introduce your idea or solution to address the need.
    - **A. Supporting point**
        - Detail
        - Detail
    - **B. Supporting point**
        - Detail
        - Detail
    - **Transition:** _____

III. Visualization (Third Main Point)

- Paint a picture of what will happen if your solution is implemented (or not implemented).
    - **A. Supporting point**
        - Detail
        - Detail
    - **B. Supporting point**
        - Detail
        - Detail
    - **Transition to Conclusion:** _____

Conclusion *(Write this section in full sentences)*

- **Restate Thesis:** _____
- **Call to Action:** _____

Bibliography (APA, MLA, or Chicago format)

Persuasive Speech – Peer Critique Form   Speaker: _____

Missing, Ineffective, Satisfactory, Good, Excellent   *Notes*

Competence	Part I: Message Preparation -- Appropriate for speaker, topic, audience, occasion, and purpose	M	I	S	G	E
Topic	Chooses and narrows a topic; Persuasive purpose					
Support/ Organization	**Introduction**– Uses attention-getter; identifies topic & persuasive thesis					
	***Persuasive appeals** – Ethos, logos, pathos					
	*Avoids logical fallacies					
	***Organization** – Uses appropriate pattern Monroe's Sequence: Need, Satisfaction, Visualization					
	Presentation aid — Design of images to persuade					
	Conclusion – Emphasizes call to **action**					
	Part II <u>Energetic</u> Message Delivery – Appropriate for audience, occasion, and purpose	M	I	S	G	E
Language	*Uses appropriate and **persuasive** language					
	*** Oral citation of sources** C1					
Voice	**Variety** – Overall variety in volume, rate, pitch & intensity to heighten and maintain interest.					
Physical Behaviors	**Movement and gestures and Appearance** – Uses movement and gestures effectively					
	Facial expression and eye contact – Overall use of facial expressiveness and eye contact to support the message and engage with listeners					
Time?						

Overall Level of Persuasion: *1: Not Persuasive*   *3: Somewhat*   *5: Very Persuasive*

Favorite part of speech?

Critiqued by _____

94 LINCOLN COSTELLO

Persuasive Speech – Peer Critique Form   Speaker: _____

Missing, Ineffective, Satisfactory, Good, Excellent   *Notes*

Competence	*Part I: Message Preparation -- Appropriate for speaker, topic, audience, occasion, and purpose*	M	I	S	G	E
Topic	Chooses and narrows a topic; Persuasive purpose					
Support/ Organization	**Introduction**– Uses attention-getter; identifies topic & persuasive thesis					
	***Persuasive appeals** – Ethos, logos, pathos					
	*Avoids logical fallacies					
	***Organization** – Uses appropriate pattern Monroe's Sequence: Need, Satisfaction, Visualization					
	Presentation aid — Design of images to persuade					
	Conclusion – Emphasizes call to **action**					
	Part II Energetic Message Delivery – Appropriate for audience, occasion, and purpose	M	I	S	G	E
Language	*Uses appropriate and **persuasive** language					
	***Oral citation of sources** C1					
Voice	**Variety** – Overall variety in volume, rate, pitch & intensity to heighten and maintain interest.					
Physical Behaviors	**Movement and gestures and Appearance** – Uses movement and gestures effectively					
	Facial expression and eye contact – Overall use of facial expressiveness and eye contact to support the message and engage with listeners					
Time?						

Overall Level of Persuasion: 1: Not Persuasive   3: Somewhat   5: Very Persuasive

Favorite part of speech?

Critiqued by _____

Persuasive Speech – Peer Critique Form   Speaker: _____

Missing, Ineffective, Satisfactory, Good, Excellent   *Notes*

Competence	Part I: Message Preparation -- Appropriate for speaker, topic, audience, occasion, and purpose	M	I	S	G	E
Topic	Chooses and narrows a topic; Persuasive purpose					
Support/ Organization	**Introduction**– Uses attention-getter; identifies topic & persuasive thesis					
	***Persuasive appeals** – Ethos, logos, pathos					
	*Avoids logical fallacies					
	***Organization** – Uses appropriate pattern Monroe's Sequence: Need, Satisfaction, Visualization					
	Presentation aid — Design of images to persuade					
	Conclusion – Emphasizes call to **action**					
	Part II Energetic Message Delivery – Appropriate for audience, occasion, and purpose	M	I	S	G	E
Language	*Uses appropriate and **persuasive** language					
	*ns**Oral citation of sources** C1					
Voice	**Variety** – Overall variety in volume, rate, pitch & intensity to heighten and maintain interest.					
Physical Behaviors	**Movement and gestures and Appearance** – Uses movement and gestures effectively					
	Facial expression and eye contact – Overall use of facial expressiveness and eye contact to support the message and engage with listeners					
Time?						

Overall Level of Persuasion: 1: Not Persuasive   3: Somewhat   5: Very Persuasive

Favorite part of speech?

Critiqued by _____

98 LINCOLN COSTELLO